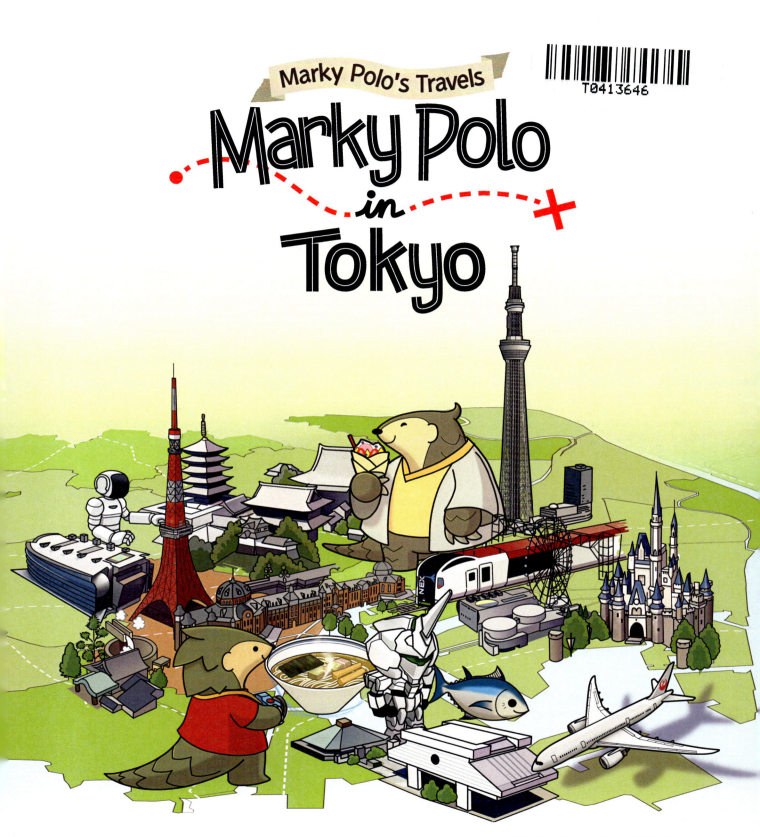

Marky Polo's Travels

Marky Polo in Tokyo

WRITTEN BY **EMILY LIM-LEH** • ILLUSTRATED BY **NICHOLAS LIEM**

A Guide to Experiencing Augmented Reality in This Book

1.  Download WSE+ app.

2.  Activate by scanning this book's barcode. Then, tap on the book cover image on your screen.

3.  Wherever you see this icon, scan the whole page.

SnapLearn is compatible with devices running minimally on iOS 8 and Android 5.0 with gyroscope. For the best AR experience, please scan the physical or PDF version of the book. For any app-related issues, please contact us via email at hello@snaplearn.com.

Powered By: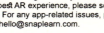

Dear Travel Diary,

I come from a line of famous travellers. Our family adopts first names based on what each of us is good at:

My great-grandparents are fearless adventurer Macho Polo and top martial arts fighter Muay-Thai Polo.

My grandparents are Matcha and Miso Polo, top experts on Japanese tea and seasoning.

My parents are Masala and Mala Polo, the largest collectors of spices in the world.

And me? I live in Singapore. I have never travelled out of the country.

My cousin Munchie Polo has just asked me to visit him in Tokyo. Yikes! Am I ready for my first trip?

Marky Polo
(Trying to make my mark in the world...
Mark my words, I will discover what I am good at!)

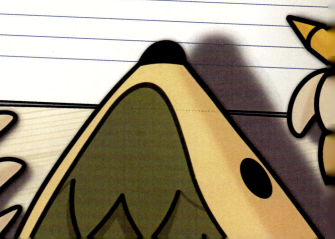

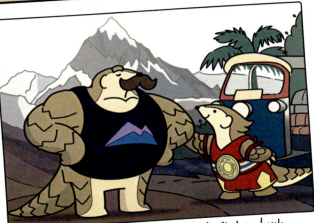

Great-grandfather **Macho Polo** — the first and only pangolin to scale to the top of Mount Everest. He met his match in great-grandmother **Muay-Thai Polo**, top martial arts fighter from Thailand.

Grandfather **Matcha Polo** and Grandmother **Miso Polo** discovered their love for Japan when they travelled there. Matcha Polo became an expert in green tea and Miso Polo an expert in Japanese food seasoning.

Father **Masala Polo** travelled to India and built up the largest spice collection in the world there. Mother **Mala Polo** shares his love of spices, but of the spicy, Sichuan tongue-numbing kind, from her China travels.

Munchie Polo — the most accomplished eater in the family, able to munch on something all the time.

Marky Polo — Never travelled, good at ...? It's still a question mark.

Marky Polo the pangolin was travelling overseas for the first time.
He was going to visit his cousin Munchie Polo in Japan.
Marky was excited, jumpy... and clueless.

Marky's first plane ride was bumpy. He survived.

But he wasn't in the best shape when he landed in Tokyo.

"Marky!" Munchie Polo called, as he munched on his food.

"'Yōkoso' means 'Welcome!' in Japanese," Munchie said.

When they reached the Tokyo Skytree, Marky and Munchie saw Crane heading to the top of the tower.

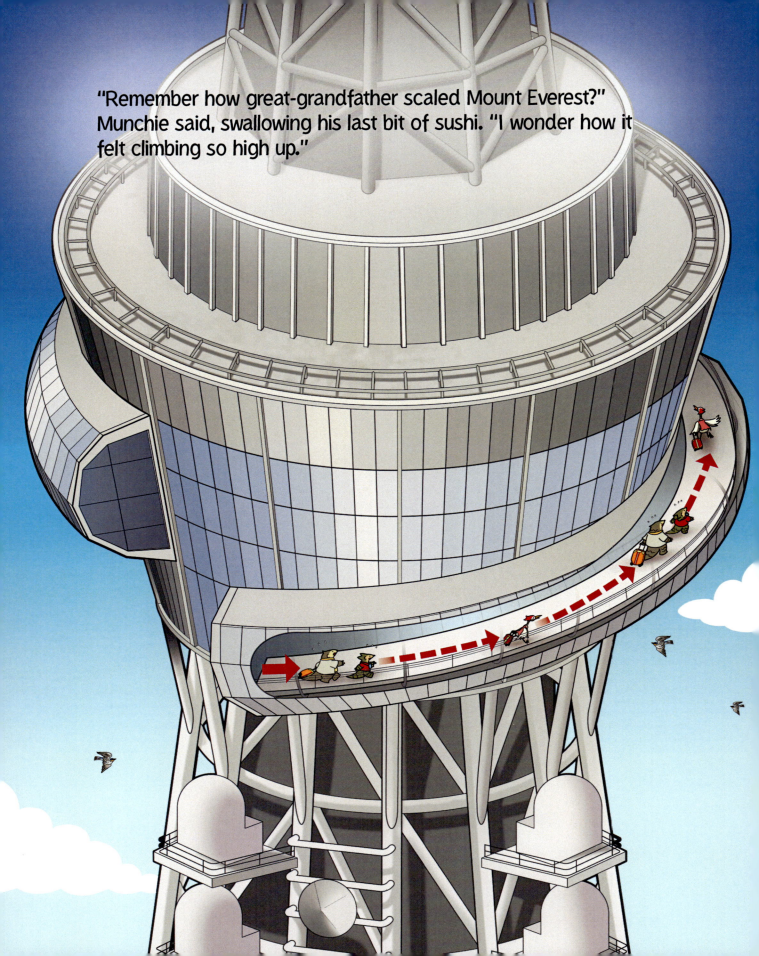

"Remember how great-grandfather scaled Mount Everest?" Munchie said, swallowing his last bit of sushi. "I wonder how it felt climbing so high up."

Marky peered down from the top of the tower.
He felt dizzy at that height.

"Urghh... Where is she going now?" Marky asked.

Kar-r-r-ooo!

Marky and Munchie followed Crane through the Gardens of the Imperial Palace.

They chased after Crane down the streets of Harajuku.

Harajuku, Tokyo's funky fashion capital, is where Japan's kawaii (cute) culture began and still thrives.

"This high-speed chase is making me hungry," Munchie said. He stopped to buy candyfloss.

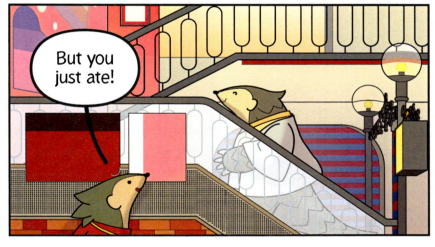

But you just ate!

They trailed Crane to the very crowded and gigantic Shibuya crossing.

Shibuya Crossing is believed to be the world's busiest scramble intersection, which sees up to a few thousand people crossing in all directions.

Hachiko's statue was built in memory of the faithful Akita dog that waited at Shibuya Station every day for its deceased owner for 10 years, till its own death.

She went that way!

"We've really lost her," Marky said with a sigh.

"Let's just go back to my apartment," Munchie said. "I'm sure you'll fit nicely into my clothes."

"Err... okay," Marky said.

They went to Shinjuku district, where Munchie lived. There, they passed the Samurai Museum.

Marky's eyes widened. "Wow, I really want to see this!"

The Samurai Museum is located in Shinjuku district, which has the world's busiest station, with over 3.4 million users daily.

  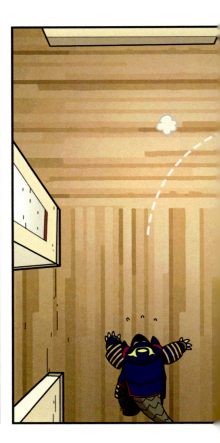

Marky looked around. He spotted Crane and chased after her.

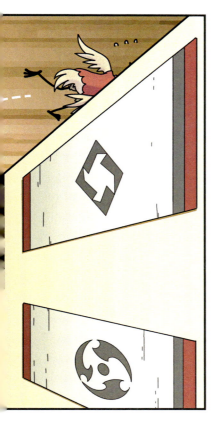

They ran straight into samurais fighting ninjas.

Marky skidded to a stop but lost his balance.

He curled up into a ball to break his fall. He rolled forward and knocked down the ninjas like bowling pins.

The audience burst into deafening applause.

After the rousing end to the show, everyone wanted to take photos with the rolling samurai with ninja moves.

Crane was in the queue too.

"I'm a visiting museum director," Crane said. "I didn't know you were part of this show! I thought you were chasing me."

Marky blushed. "Actually, I have been chasing you since we mixed up our trolley bags at the airport."

"Ah... Kar-r-r-ooo!" Crane said. "I am so sorry! Please let me make it up to you. If you are free tomorrow, I would like to take you around Tokyo."

After his madcap first day in Tokyo, Marky only wanted to go shopping the next day.

So, Crane brought Marky and Munchie to a few shopping areas.

Marky gushed at the toys at Tokyo Character Street.

He drooled over plastic miniatures of Japanese food.
He got carried away by the cosplay masks and costumes.

But why buy fake food when you can have real food?

Green tea has so many health benefits!

Marky went wacky over manga comics and trading cards at Akihabara.

Watching sumo wrestling morning practice

Sensō-ji, Tokyo's oldest temple

Tsukiji Fish Market

teamLab Borderless (world's first digital art museum)

At an onsen (hot water spring)

Tokyo Disneyland

Fun facts on some animals native to Japan:

See if you can spot these local animals in the story!

Japanese red-crowned crane

Red-crowned cranes are one of the world's largest cranes. A fully-grown adult stands at five feet, with a wingspan that grows to eight feet. The crane's long-coiled windpipe allows it to trumpet so loudly it can be heard more than a mile away. These cranes are a symbol of love, happiness and good luck in Japan.

Amami rabbit

The Amami rabbit is often called a living fossil, as it descended from ancient rabbits that once lived on the mainland. It is now only found on the islands of Amami and Tokuno.

Japanese macaque

The Japanese macaque is also known as the Snow Monkey. It can survive in cold weather as low as 5 degrees Fahrenheit and can also be found soaking in hot springs. Other than humans, it is the only other animal known to wash its food before eating it!

Akita-Inu and Shiba-Inu

Akita-Inu

The Akita-Inu is a very popular Japanese dog breed and a cultural symbol of Japan. Hachiko, the world's most famous Akita dog, is fondly remembered for its faithfulness to its owner. A statue marks the same spot where it waited 10 years for its owner who had passed away.

Shiba-Inu

The Shiba-Inu is one of Japan's native dog breeds. Previously a hunting dog, the intelligent, good-natured Shiba is the most popular Japanese companion dog. Shibas are known for their spirited nature, small upright ears and cat-like agility.

Now let's learn more about pangolins:

Marky Polo is a Sunda pangolin, the most common species of pangolins in Asia.

The pangolin is sometimes called "scaly anteater" as it is covered in an armour of scales. If threatened, it rolls up into a ball, using its sharp scales on its tail to defend itself. It has a long snout and tongue for slurping up ants and termites. Sunda pangolins are critically endangered. They are hunted illegally for their flesh and scales.

Pangolin

For my son Caleb, who inspired Marky Polo
and contributed great ideas to this story
—E.L.

For Phoebe, Jaden, and Karen with love
—N.L.

Published by
WS Education, an imprint of
World Scientific Publishing Co. Pte. Ltd.
5 Toh Tuck Link, Singapore 596224
USA office: 27 Warren Street, Suite 401-402, Hackensack, NJ 07601
UK office: 57 Shelton Street, Covent Garden, London WC2H 9HE

National Library Board, Singapore Cataloguing in Publication Data
Name(s): Lim, Emily, 1971–   . | Liem, Nicholas, illustrator.
Title: Marky Polo in Tokyo / written by Emily Lim-Leh ; illustrated by Nicholas Liem.
Other title: Marky Polo's travels ; Volume 1.
Description: Singapore : WS Education, 2021.
Identifier(s): OCN 1225976737 | ISBN 978-981-12-3389-0 (paperback) | 978-981-12-3266-4 (hardcover)
Subject(s): LCSH: Pangolins--Juvenile fiction. | Tokyo (Japan)--Juvenile fiction.
Classification: DDC 428.6--dc23

British Library Cataloguing-in-Publication Data
A catalogue record for this book is available from the British Library.

Text copyright ©2021 by Emily Lim-Leh
Illustration copyright ©2021 by Nicholas Liem
All rights reserved. This book, or parts thereof, may not be reproduced in any form or by any means, electronic or mechanical, including photocopying, recording or any information storage and retrieval system now known or to be invented, without written permission from the publisher.

For photocopying of material in this volume, please pay a copying fee through the Copyright Clearance Center, Inc., 222 Rosewood Drive, Danvers, MA 01923, USA. In this case permission to photocopy is not required from the publisher.

Desk Editor: Daniele Lee

Printed in Singapore

Look out for more dynamic, full-colour illustrated children's books in this exciting series "Marky Polo's Travels". Enriched by Augmented Reality, Marky Polo takes on Beijing and Singapore next!

To receive updates about children's titles from WS Education, go to https://www.worldscientific.com/page/newsletter/subscribe, choose "Education", click on "Children's Books" and key in your email address.